GENERATIONAL
CURSES

Family Circle of
GENERATIONAL CURSES

Minoka SMITH

XULON PRESS

Xulon Press
2301 Lucien Way #415
Maitland, FL 32751
407.339.4217
www.xulonpress.com

Photo by BLive Photography
www.blivephotography.com

Lance McCoy photographer
Email: Lance@blivephotography.com
Phone number: 443-983-5874

Hair stylist Ashley Digss
Email: stash102116@yahoo.com
Phone number: 410- 999-4934

Makeup Artist Shawn Ferebee
Email: Scarlet.muse70@gmail.com
Phone number: 443-418-8493

Unless otherwise indicated, Scripture quotations taken from the King James Version (KJV) – *public domain.*

Printed in the United States of America.

ISBN-13: 978-1-6305-0190-7

DEDICATION AND ACKNOWLEGMENTS

"I can do all things through Christ which strengtheneth me" (Philippians 4:13 KJV).

I dedicate this book to the son of God for giving me the strength and faith to believe in myself and share my story. I hope my testimony will help others recognize that generational cures and spiritual warfare are real. I pray my book blesses you and ministers to your heart and mind.

To my parents: Lagranda Delvinia Smith and my late father Leon Yancey Smith. I love and cherish you both. Thank you for making me the woman I am today.

To my three amazing, gifted, smart, and talented children: Ayonna Wallace, Gerald Saunders, Jr., and Triran Saunders, all of you are a blessing to my life. Your love and support has motivated me to never give up on my dreams! You also inspire me to create change in the world. Stay connected to one another and to God. I pray that when you read this book you will experience spiritual growth and allow God to order your steps.

> "⁶As ye have therefore received Christ Jesus
> the Lord, so walk ye in him: ⁷Rooted and
> built up in him, and stablished in the faith,
> as ye have been taught, abounding therein
> with thanksgiving" (Col. 2:6-7).

To my beloved brothers: William Clark and Tony Mobley, I truly love you both. I hope your lives will be blessed through reading my book. Thank you for always believing in me.

To my great niece: India Lee, you are my angel and the apple of my eye. Let God continue to order your steps. Trust Him with all your heart. Stay confident in who you are! You have a lot to offer the world!

To all of my nieces and nephews, may God bless you and your families. Always believe in yourself and follow your dreams. Don't allow the enemy to stop you from fulfilling God's purpose for your life. Remember you are filled with wisdom, vision, knowledge, and power. I pray as you read this book, it will bless your life.

To my children's fathers: Gerald Saunders and Larry Andre Wallace, you are extraordinary fathers! I thank God for both of you. Thank you for being a part of my journey and always having my back.

To all of my godchildren, you have been a blessing to me! We have shared beautiful moments together. I am proud of who all of you have become. Thank you for allowing me to be a part of your journey. May my life lessons continue to direct your paths in life.

To my godmothers: Barbara Hawkes, Carlena Dixon, and Brenda Chase, you are phenomenal women of God who possess strength, grace, class, and swag. I appreciate all of you for being an advocate, friend, and confidant in my life. Thank you for helping me become the woman God has called me to be.

To my godfather: Raymond Casey, Sr., thank you for your warm heart and words of wisdom. There's never a dull moment that your laughter doesn't light up the room. You may fuss, cuss, or stomp, but you always open your heart to those close to you! You are a wonderful friend and father. I am blessed and honored to have you as my godfather! I'll always love you!

To my children's grandmother: Ms. Martina Thomas, thank you for being a God-fearing woman. I could not have asked for a better grandmother. Your love is unconditional. Thank you for always being there for me and your grandchildren. I will always cherish you! You are a phenomenal woman.

To Author Christopher Allen, Marlon Harty, Brent S. Marble, Craig Graves, Sr., Lonyett Michael, Danielle Bethea, Latonya Savage, Lori Gee, Jeffrey Shepherd, Kiesha Byers, April Harris, Lisa Thomas, Michelle Whitby, Frank Martin, Gerald D. Jackson, and Mr. Peewee, a special thanks to all of you for walking beside me on this journey. When I expressed that I was going to write a book, you didn't think it was a crazy idea. You always cheered me on with encouraging words, love, and support. I thank God for allowing me to have a strong connection with you all. You are the best! I am grateful that you held me accountable to finish writing this book.

I have to start by thanking my awesome mentor, author Cheryle T. Ricks, for believing in me when I wanted to give up! There were moments when I wanted to toss this book across the room from being so frustrated. With your warm smile and sense of humor, you had a way of making the process easier to keep pressing forward. Writing a book is harder than I thought. It is not an overnight task. But more rewarding than I could have ever imagined. Without God and you, none of this would have been possible. Writing about my life story was a surreal process. I am forever indebted to you for supporting me. It is because of your efforts that I am able to have a legacy to pass on to my family. Thank you for your love, support, understanding, and for helping me to develop into a successful author. You will forever be my beautiful angel and dearest friend! I thank God for you!

In remembrance of: Denzel Sarbeng, Nathaniel Eugene Porter, Juwan Vellines, Kalltyree, you will forever be in my heart! May God continue to strengthen and bless your families with love, joy, and peace!

To my special friend: Miss Linda Jones, I will miss you my friend. I can't believe you are gone! We bonded in a short period of time. I will miss your beautiful smile and the talks we shared about life. You were a divine being with a heart of gold. I did it, Linda! I finished my book. I know you would have been proud of me. I love you, woman of God!

If there is anyone I didn't mention, thank you for sharing a part of my journey!

TABLE OF CONTENTS

Foreword By Author Cheryle T. Ricks

I was fortunate to meet Minoka at a youth event. She and I were both guest speakers for that event. One day she shared that she was writing her first book. We realized that the true purpose for our meeting was to birth this book.

Minoka faced several obstacles while writing this book. I watched this awesome lady grow into a woman of conviction. She is determined, focused, and passionate about helping other people successfully overcome the challenges in their life.

Many people will be able to relate to this book. It will allow them to know that they are not alone. They will learn that the pain and heartache they suffer is the fuel that moves them into the purpose that God has for their life.

This book will give people the road map they need to overcome the challenges they face. People everywhere will be sharing this book with other people, so that they too can get the blessing God has for them in this amazing book!

Introduction

When I was a seed in my mother's belly, the Devil already had a plot against my life to keep me from reaching my full potential. I remember meeting three women when I was about twenty years old. They prophesied over me about the plans God had for my life. They stated that I needed to stay connected to God and be careful of who I brought into my life. They explained that I was very gifted, and the adversary was going to use distractions in every way he could to keep me from using the gifts God blessed me with. When they were praying over me, it felt strange. They prayed a powerful prayer of protection over my life. After they prayed for me, I attended church regularly, and I didn't hang out in clubs. I was a homebody connected to God and my family.

Since that time, my life has been filled with many ups and downs. I remembered when I was growing up, my family seemed to go through a lot of things in their lives. I couldn't understand why they kept repeating the same patterns. It was destroying their lives. I loved them so much, but I didn't understand them. The Devil had them trapped in their minds and stuck in the past. As time went on, I often wondered why there was a dark cloud over my family. It wasn't until I got hurt on my job and had to retire that I realized there was a generational curse over my family. My family didn't have a close relationship with God, which left them open for the adversary to do his work in their lives.

These cruses hindered us from growing and reaching what God destined us to be. It just wasn't normal to me. How could something you couldn't see have so much power and control over one family. I loved my children and family very much. Because of my relationship with God, I realized that it was important for me to help other families recognize generational cruses in their families, so their children and grandchildren wouldn't be affected by the adversary's crafty tricks, schemes, and attacks over their lives.

I am writing this book to help others understand the generational curses in their families and to help them overcome the tricks and attacks that the adversary uses to keep them from reaching their full potential and purpose God ordained before they were born. Some of the tactics the adversary uses are drug abuse, alcohol abuse, failed marriages, adultery, anger, control, jealousy, selfishness, depression, and incarceration. Before each of us was born, God created a plan and purpose for our lives to be a great representation of Him. When the adversary sees there is a chosen one, he comes to steal, kill, and destroy. He starts with the parents by attacking them in their minds, spirit, and bodies. When he succeeds, he then goes after the children because he knows they will do great things to achieve what their parents could not. His goal is to keep them distracted and not allow them to get to the next level in their lives. Curses are repeated from generation to generation as noted in Exodus 34:7:

> Keeping mercy for thousands, forgiving iniquity and transgression and sin, and that will by no means clear the guilty; visiting the iniquity of the fathers upon the children, and upon the children's children, unto the third and to the fourth generation.

However, if you are struggling in your life and you are wondering why you are fighting the same situations that you faced as a child, you are experiencing a generational curse that is trying to keep you in bondage. The enemy is trying to program you with doubt, fear, jealousy, anger and depression. God's purpose is for you to win, and the adversary's purpose is to keep you shackled. Through my story, I pray that you are healed and delivered as you read how I fought my way through the attacks of the adversary. He tried to divide my family with chaos and confusion. You can use this book as a guide to help you and your family overcome the generational cruses that you may have. Whatever applies to you, let it help you to live your God-given purpose. This will keep you spiritually connected to God, and it will allow you to help your children stay connected to God. It will protect their minds, so the adversary cannot tempt them with the evilness and distractions like social media, games systems, and TV programs. I have made it through the fire and broken the generational cruses on my family. If it wasn't for the blood of Jesus and his undying love for me, I wouldn't be the God-fearing woman I am today. I can now fulfill my purpose and walk in my gifts and talents. I am leaving a legacy behind for my children to follow.

> "For thou art an holy people unto the LORD thy God, and the Lord hath chosen thee to be a peculiar people unto himself, above all the nations that are upon the earth," (Deut. 14:2).

1

MY FIRST LOVE

One day, we had a terrible snowstorm, and our car broke down. Thank goodness we had a first aid kit, water, flash lights, and blankets just in case something like this would happen. My dad had to wrap my mom in covers and carry me on his shoulders. It was the worst blizzard of the year. It was so cold, and the snow was up to our knees. We began walking home, but my mom couldn't walk any further. My dad put my mom back in the car. He took a chance and carried me the five miles home. He left me with a neighbor, and he ran all the way back to the car to rescue my mom. I was so upset. I didn't know if I would ever see my parents again. It was really bad! The news told everyone to stay in because it was very dangerous. Our neighbor, Mr. Jim, found my parents about 7:30 the next morning. They were so cold and sick. Mr. Jim got them out of those wet cold clothes into something warm. My dad kept his arms around my mom all night. My dad was thanking God that we were all safe even though we had lost our car.

The next day came, and we were able to return to our house. My dad returned to work, and my mom attended to me. There was no school for a few weeks. My dad had to go in to work for just a few hours. There were machines and other mechanical issues that had to be dealt with because of the weather freezing the pipes. My dad and his coworkers had to carpool using the church's van to get to work. I stared out the window at all of that snow. The streetlights were off, and it was quiet with no human movement.

As time went on, things began to clear up. Life was finally getting back to normal. The streets were being cleaned; the market was open again. People were enjoying life as if there were no tragic snow storm. Finally, my mom returned to work, and I went back to school. I couldn't wait for Fridays; since the snow was clearing, we could go back to Roy Rogers. They had the best biscuits in the world. After that, I would go home to see my favorite TV shows, Dukes of Hazards and Knots Landing. I know I was a little young to be watching those shows, but I loved them.

One day, I got a bad stomach ache. My dad was a hilarious person. He went to the store and bought some ice cream, knowing I couldn't eat it. We would cuddle in front of the TV, and my dad would make jokes saying, "Squirrel, don't you want to try daddy ice cream?" I would cry and run into my room asking my dad to stop teasing me. I thought to myself, *When I feel better, I can choose any ice cream I want.*

Later the next day, my dad and I were playing board games, but he stopped to smoke a cigar and drink a beer. I had never seen my dad do that before. I climbed up in my daddy's lap and said, "Daddy, what are those things you are putting in your mouth, and what are you drinking?" He said, "You shouldn't be around me while I am having them." I told my dad, "I don't want you to smoke or drink because it is bad for you. I don't want you to die." He laughed and said, "Okay, Squirrel, Daddy won't smoke or drink anymore." I really think he continued but just not around me.

I told my dad, "I don't want you to smoke or drink because it is bad for you. I don't want you to die." He laughed and said, "Okay, Squirrel, Daddy won't smoke or drink anymore." I really think he continued but just not around me.

It was a hot summer day. My mom and dad were preparing to go to my father's music studio where he played jazz with his band. I would hear them playing in the studio, and I would dance all over the room. I had to wait until they got half way through some of their songs before I could go in the studio. I became curious and wandered into the studio trying to see my dad. I smelled something really strange, but I didn't know what it was. Whatever it was it smelled really good. My dad and his friends were smoking something weird. My mom rushed in the room and pulled me out of the studio. She was very upset, and she started fussing at my dad. I don't know what the misunderstanding between them was, but my dad came out and apologized to me, although I didn't really understand why. I later learned that my dad and his friend were smoking marijuana. That evening, we ate dinner with my dad, all the musicians, and their mates. There was lots of food, music, playing, and singing at the table; such a great moment!

As the night went on, my dad, my mom, and I left to go home to get ready for church. We were all active in the church. My mom sung in choir, my dad was a deacon, and I sung in children choir and attended Bible study. My church friends and I would sit in the choir area and pass notes back and forth while everyone in the church was getting the Holy Ghost, screaming, and shouting. We had so much fun keeping ourselves entertained. But, when my Pastor would begin to preach, we would all stop and listen. He really captured our attention. Sometimes I understood what he was preaching, and at times I didn't, but my church experience was really great. After services, we would go over to my auntie's house and have Sunday dinner with all of our extend family. There was good laughter, good conversation, good music, good food, and children playing all through the house. It was good for me growing up as a child. It kept us connected as a family.

On June 22, 1982, when I was nine years old, my daddy was supposed to come home for lunch because it was our daughter-daddy time together. He worked such long hours. On this particular day, it was different. He never made it back home. I was wondering why I didn't see him all that day. Things seem strange, and it was difficult for me to play with my dolls and friends as the day went on. I would go back and forth to the window looking for him to pull up to our house, but it never happened. As the night was approaching, my mom had to get me fed, bathed, and ready for school the next day. I laid in the bed waiting for him to come home, but eventually I fell off to sleep. Something woke me out of my sleep. I saw a dark figure walk pass my bedroom door wearing a long black robe and hood with no face. I was so scared!

Soon after that, my mom came running into my room saying, "Wake up and get dressed. I just received a phone call that your dad was rushed to the hospital!" She was panicking and crying terribly while we were driving to the hospital. I asked my mom what happened to my dad. She said his job had given him a get together for his job promotion, and he was dancing and fell out on the floor.

I sat there in disbelief because I didn't see my dad all day. I told my mom that a dark figure had walked passed my bedroom door that night and it scared me. "It was a sign of death, and Daddy had a heart attack, Mommy." Mind you, we had not arrived to the hospital yet to confirm that my father had a heart attack.

She began yelling and screaming, telling me to "Stop speaking in that manner about your Daddy because it is not true." Therefore, I begin weeping about my daddy. Remember I was just nine years old, but God gave me a premonition about my father.

We finally made it to the hospital, and we sat in the waiting room for the doctor to come out to tell us how my father was doing. However, I couldn't wait any longer and ran off looking for my daddy in different hospital rooms. There was one room with the curtain closed, and you couldn't see the patient. I pulled the curtain back. It was my dad with all of these cords all over his body and a mask over his face. He was laying there and not moving at all. I walked up to him and touched his face, his hands, and his arms. His body was so warm it was a scary and devastating moment. I begin to climb up on his hospital bed beside him, but the nurse and the doctor found me and started taking me back to my mom. I was screaming and yelling, "Daddy, it's Squirrel. I don't want to leave you, Daddy, wake up."

My mom took me in her arms and said, "Daddy is gone. He is dead!"

I couldn't understand why she was saying that to me. Once we got home, I was heartbroken. The house was so quite you could hear a pin drop. Our house had a cold, lifeless feeling. My mom was in a daze because she lost her best friend. It was such a sad and lonely moment for both of us. My mom and I were not eating or sleeping very well. My mom stayed very busy making the arrangements for my dad's funeral.

When the day came to attend my father's funeral, it was so unreal seeing people my dad had worked with crying. My brothers and other family members were in so much pain. When I said my last goodbyes to my daddy, it was too much for me to handle as a child. I would no longer have my daughter-daddy time with my daddy! I wanted to see his eye looks up at me and hear his voice speak to me. I also wanted him to wake up and say, "Everything is okay, Squirrel. It was just a bad dream. Daddy is here." As the coffin was closing and being lowered in the ground, I knew that was the final goodbye. I would never see my daddy again. Because I lost my dad at a young age, it changed the positive loving foundation I had with my mom and dad. The adversary knew God's plan for my life and he set me up to have failed relationships which caused me heartache, turmoil, and disappointment. "For I know the thoughts that I think toward you, saith the LORD, thoughts of peace, and not of evil, to give you an expected end" (Jer. 29:11). I was looking for my father's love in all the wrong places. Therefore, I attracted men from broken families who didn't love themselves and couldn't love me.

Jewels to Live By:

1. If you have lost a parent or caretaker, seek God for comfort.
2. Love yourself.
3. Know your worth.
4. Don't settle for just any type of relationship or friendship.
5. Don't look for validation from anyone.
6. Seek God in everything you do.
7. Don't allow bitterness and anger to interfere with you having loving, healthy relationships with others.
8. Ask God for guidance and knowledge to make the right decisions in your life.
9. Remember, Satan is behind generational curses and the evilness in the world.

> "Wherein in time past ye walked according to the course of this world, according to the prince of the power of the air, the spirit that now worketh in the children of disobedience" (Eph. 2:2).

2

THE DARKEST MOMENT

A t eleven years old, my mom allowed a close family member to babysit me because she had to work now that my father had passed. This close family member spent a lot of time with me. She was the person who picked me up from school and attended most of my school events. After school, I would have lunch and do my homework at her home until my mom got off from work. I had a lot of fun there with her and her family. It was pretty cool. I admired her a lot! We would go outside to the playground. We did flips, played tag, and all that fun kid stuff children like to do. We had a great time. Sometimes I would spend the weekend with her and her family. We also went to church functions together. I often ate Sunday dinner at her grandmother's house. The food was delicious and everyone was so kind. They took great care of me. My mom really trusted her and believed I would be ok in her care.

One day after school though, something was different. That day we went into her room to play games and watch movies. She closed her bedroom door when she usually kept it opened. Once we finished playing games around 1:30 p.m. in the afternoon, it would be time for me to take a nap because that was the normal routine since I only had a half day at school. This day was strange! She said she wanted to show me something and told me to climb on top of her. She began kissing me in my mouth, with one hand rubbing on my back and my butt. My legs were spread apart and her hands were stroking me between my legs. She pressed her body against mine and started grinding. She told me that this is the way a man is supposed to touch, love, and kiss me. I knew that this was not right! I was only eleven years old, and it hadn't been long since my dad passed. I admired and looked up to this person and didn't understand why she was doing this to me. It made me very uncomfortable to be around her, and I didn't want her to watch me anymore. But, because I was a child, I didn't know how to express the situation to my mom. My body wasn't ready to be exposed in that way. Therefore, it made me a promiscuous and confused little girl desiring things I couldn't understand that could ruin my life growing up.

> The LORD is my light and my salvation; whom shall I fear? The LORD is the strength of my life; of whom shall I be afraid? ²When the wicked, even mine enemies and my foes, came upon me to

eat up my flesh, they stumbled and fell.
(Psalm 27:1-2)

Knowing what I experienced, please be careful of who you trust your children with. There are people who are predators of young children. It is imperative that you have all the information about who is caring for your child, even family members and close friends:

> Envyings, murders, drunkenness, revellings, and such like: of the which I tell you before, as I have also told you in time past, that they which do such things shall not inherit the kingdom of God. (Galatians 5:21)

It is a painful situation when someone has sexually abused your child. It causes them to have problems throughout out their childhood and adulthood. The following are some of the uncontrollable behaviors that

Knowing what I experienced, please be careful of who you trust your children with. There are people who are predators of young children. It is imperative that you have all the information about who is caring for your child, even family members and close friends.

could happen if you or your child was sexually abused: masturbation with toys and animals, aggressive behaviors towards other children, substance abuse, and children being socially withdrawn from other people. It is your obligation as a parent to invest time with your children. "Train up a child in the way he should go: and when he is old, he will not depart from it" (Prov. 22:6).

Losing my father had a great impact on my life and my family. He was my first true love and the rock of my family.

Not having my father changed me and my family in so many ways. I hardly saw my brothers. They were always running the streets of Baltimore, never making any time for me. Coping with the pain of losing my dad wasn't good for me growing up, and I couldn't bring him back. I had no control over God calling my dad home. I resented God and my mom. I hated my mom and wished she was dead. I took all of my anger and frustrations out on my mom. I was disrespectful, argumentative, and not performing well in school. I even ran away from home. Finding my way as a teenager was difficult because when I was younger I always had my dad to turn to for everything. He was my guide and the driving force in my life and my only example of a good man. My brothers only

> *Losing my father had a great impact on my life and my family. He was my first true love and the rock of my family.*

showed me the negative, cheating, and disrespectful ways of a man.

Jewels to Live By:

1. It is important that you show your children love through hugs and support.
2. Have family dinners and talks with your children. This will keep you connected with your children.
3. Don't show your children love only through giving them material possessions.
4. Once you lose precious time with them, you won't get it back! In doing these jewels, you will protect their innocence.

3

THE REBELLIOUS
ADOLESCENT

My mother was not a very affectionate person. She was very controlling, and we didn't spend a lot of time together, except when she was trying to make me a superstar, which made me very resentful towards her. I wanted to make more decisions about what I participated in. Therefore, I became very rebellious, and I looked to others for advice. My mom put me in Sunday school, modeling, dance, and acting in church and in school. But, I wanted to play sports and just be a child.

I started middle school at fourteen years old. I was quiet and stayed to myself, not really connecting with other children my ages. I couldn't go over to any of my friends' houses because my mother was very controlling. My godfather would talk with my mom about keeping me sheltered. He felt that it was not a healthy lifestyle for me after all I had been through.

My mom started letting me go out more. I was excited to see all of the inner city youth my age coming out to the skating rink. I was making new friends and hanging out. My life wasn't boring anymore. Therefore, my mom allowed me to go every Saturday with my god-father. That was the best part of my life! I was on top of the world and free.

> "Restore to me the joy of Your salvation,
> And uphold me *by Your* generous Spirit,"
> (Ps. 51:12).

My home life improved a lot, but my school life did not. In school, I was picked on and teased because I was different. The friends I thought I had betrayed me. They joined a group of girls who were making fun of me. Going to school was a nightmare! I just

That was the best part of my life! I was on top of the world and free.

didn't fit in. I got into a terrible fight with other girls. I also experienced prejudice from some of the Caucasian students who tried to rape me in the classroom, but I fought them off. After that incident, my mother transferred me out of that school.

I didn't attend school dances or school trips. My mom kept me busy teaching me how to manage household responsibilities. She wanted me to know how to take care of things if something would happen to her.

My mom gave me a lot of exposure by allowing me to travel to other parts of the country, so I could see life beyond where I lived.

I had my first boyfriend when I was in the ninth grade. He was a football player who lived in Baltimore City. Our relationship was good until I became pregnant. I contacted him to let him know that I was pregnant. He told me to have an abortion because he was on his way to college on a football scholarship. He also stated that the pregnancy would jeopardize his current relationship, and he was sorry that it happened. I was very hurt and disappointed. I was scared because I had never been pregnant before. I noticed changes in my skin and body.

My mom was furious when she found out that I was pregnant. I had so much going for myself with modeling and my acting career. My grades dropped terribly in school. I was so ashamed, hurt, and embarrassed that I cried out for my dad. I knew if he was living I would not have become pregnant. My mom and cousin took me out of Maryland to have an abortion. It was a disgrace to be pregnant at fourteen years old in those days. The abortion was the most unbearable pain I ever experienced in my life. I felt terrible knowing that I killed a human being who didn't ask to be here. I

I felt terrible knowing that I killed a human being who didn't ask to be here.

had to live with that decision the rest of my life. I found out later that my mom had gotten pregnant at the age of fifteen. I realized that a generational cruse was passed down to me:

I found out later that my mom had gotten pregnant at the age of fifteen. I realized that a generational cruse was passed down to me.

Keeping mercy for thousands, forgiving iniquity and transgression and sin, and that will by no means clear the guilty; visiting the iniquity of the fathers upon the children, and upon the children's children, unto the third and to the fourth, generation. (Exodus 34:7)

As time when on, I became a promiscuous teenager and began having more sexual relationships. I used my looks and charm to get whatever I wanted from men. Sometimes, the outcome was not beneficial to me. If you are reading my story, I want you to understand what it means to be a promiscuous person through the "Jewels to Live By."

---

*I became a promiscuous
teenager and began having
more sexual relationships.
I used my looks and charm
to get whatever I wanted
from men.*

Jewels to Live By:

1. You will experience not loving yourself and not knowing your self-worth.
2. Please know that you are loved!
3. You will feel unworthy if you use your body for love, attention, or material gain.
4. If you do those sinful behaviors, you will miss God's will for your life.
5. You need to be your authentic self.
6. Otherwise you allow the adversary to attack you with hurt and pain, and you will never have a fulfilled relationship.
7. Wait on God to send you your mate because you will be a priority to that person without using your body.

4

New Beginnings

On September 22, 1989, when I was about sixteen years old, my mom and I moved to Baltimore, Maryland, to finish my eleventh-grade year in Baltimore public schools. I didn't like the area we moved to. I loved living in the country of Howard County with woods, lakes, and rivers, and I was used to living in a diverse community with different races. Baltimore wasn't as diverse as Howard County. The people in Baltimore were predominately African Americans. It was a congested and polluted city. There were no open spaces or lakes or rivers. The homes were too small and built close together. Baltimore was a fast moving city, and it was hard for me to keep up.

When I started school, it was crazy! The students were loud in the hallways and unfriendly. They gave me mean looks and called me all kinds of horrible names. This was a big adjustment for me, and I just wasn't ready for that change in my life. As the school year continued, I began to make friends with three young ladies who were creative, smart, and fun. We had a lot in common, and we would spend time after school talking about our aspirations and dreams of going to college and becoming successful young women.

I acquired a lot from high school. I was in the nursing program and the debate team class, and I loved debating about different topics. My friends were in some of the same programs. We were pretty mature and had our own style, and because of this, each of us brought something different to our friendship. We all possessed certain intellectual views. One of my friends was very brainy, the other friend was very funny and a jokester, and the third friend was very outspoken about things in life and analyzed everything. She was a straight A-student. We were so close that we were each other's dates to the prom, where we laughed, danced, and partied all night long, taking pictures and making school memories. I miss those days. I can honestly say those friendships were the best I ever had. We were the only four female seniors accepted to out-of-state colleges.

After graduating high school, my relationship with my mom got a whole lot better. We spent time doing more things together as a family. She treated me as an adult with love, and she supported my goals and aspirations. I also worked full time at a shoe store as an assistant manager to save money for college. I made good money and learned how to be a great business woman. Unfortunately, after a year of being in college, I could no longer attend college because of life circumstances.

About a year later, I decide to become an entrepreneur, and, with the support of my mom, I opened my own day care center. Working with the children and teaching them to be knowledgeable and smart was a pleasure. I incorporated field trips, mentoring programs, and prepared them for their new journey in school. The parents were wonderful, hardworking young men and women who worked to ensure that their children would be successful in life.

While running my day care center, I reconnected with a guy from high school who had a crush on me. He was so funny, and he had a personality out of this world. However, I knew if I dated him, we wouldn't be an item too long because of his popularity, but I dated him anyway. One evening, while having dinner together I told him that I had missed my period (menstrual cycle) and I think I am pregnant.

I didn't want any children. I knew that being pregnant would interfere with everything I had going for myself and my dreams. I was twenty-three years old, and it was just the wrong time. When I took the pregnancy test, it confirmed that I was pregnant. I decided to have my baby because the doctor stated that it would be dangerous for me and my baby if I had an abortion. I then moved back home with my mom. I continued running my day care center. Unfortunately, it didn't work out with my baby's father because he wasn't mature enough for the responsibilities of parenthood. We continued to have a good friendship for our new bundle of joy we were bringing in the world. We gave birth to a beautiful baby girl on December 29, 1992. I stayed focus on being a mom and business women.

My life began to change quickly. I began hanging out in clubs and attending bisexual and homosexual parties. Because I came from such a sheltered life, I began smoking marijuana and drinking alcohol. This is where the generational cruse of substance abuse began repeating itself with me.

> [15] Love not the world, neither the things that are in the world. If any man love the world, the love of the Father is not in him. [16] For all that is in the world, the lust of the flesh, and the lust of the eyes, and the pride of life, is not of the Father, but is of the world. (1 John 2:15-16)

Remember, my dad drank and smoked marijuana. You have to pay close attention to your family history to identify reoccurring problems and repeated failures in your life. For example: No ambition, no vision, no direction, and ungodly patterns.

This is where the generational cruse of substance abuse began repeating itself with me.

Jewels to Live By:

1. No matter the distractions the Devil throws your way, stay on the path that God has you on. Distraction is a trick of the Devil to delay you and get your eyes off of God.
2. Be mindful of who you spend most of your time with. They can be a blessing or a hindrance.

5

WALKING INTO WOMANHOOD

Seven years later, I married my best friend. He was the sweetest guy I have ever met. He owned his own body oil and photography business. We were a power couple. I owned my own daycare business, and I was a successful make-up artist. I also taught at a modeling agency. On July 15, 1999, we had twin boys. We were a beautiful family. I couldn't have asked for a better marriage.

Four years later, things began to shift in our marriage. My husband lost both of his businesses due to spending so much time with his friends and getting high on marijuana. We began to have arguments, and we stopped sleeping together. Our family was becoming divided. I was trying to keep both of my businesses afloat, which put more pressure on me. He was not making himself useful as husband and father. My children and I were suffering. I was disappointed because that was not the kind of marriage I wanted. I went back to college part-time to study business administration. I closed my daycare center and continued my make-up business. I was losing everything, my marriage, and my business. The Devil was on my trail.

My husband and I didn't marry for the right reasons. We moved too quickly. He was this handsome guy that I had a great friendship with. I really didn't know him as a person. I assumed he was the same guy I knew when I was younger. We should have gone before God about our relationship. We didn't take the time to find out about our relationship with God. We took a lot for granted. When I had my sons, I no longer wanted to smoke marijuana or hang out at parties. I was becoming a family woman. My husband continued to smoke marijuana and go to parties, which caused arguments, fights, and adultery in our marriage. If your relationship with God isn't right, don't start any relationship. You will open the door to confusion, regrets, and not knowing the meaning of true love.

Marriage is very serious. It is a permanent commitment between a man, a woman, and God. "Therefore shall a man leave his father and his mother, and shall cleave unto his wife: and they shall be one flesh" (Gen. 2:24). This means you should not treat one another with disrespect, physical, or verbal abuse and no infidelity. There is no 101 class about love and marriage except what God has written in His Word. You cannot just abandon one another or be emotionally unavailable. You have to ask for God's help and work through it. Make sure your partner has his or her own relationship with God.

---

*If your relationship with
God isn't right, don't start
any relationship. You will
open the door to confusion,
regrets, and not knowing the
meaning of true love.*

Jewels to Live By:

1. Seek God before you make a decision about marriage.
2. Don't have sex before marriage.
3. Don't rush into relationships.
4. Give yourself time to know who you are.
5. Make sure you keep God in the center of your life.
6. Know God's plan and purpose for your life.
7. Attend counseling with your partner before marriage.
8. Make sure you and your partner are financially stable.
9. Make sure that you and your partner share the same values, beliefs, and religion.
10. Keep people out of your business.
11. Have married couples as friends.
12. Talk with your partner about parenthood, whether you have children or plan to have children.
13. Always pray together.
14. Love yourself first before trying to love someone else.

15. Don't bring old habits, such as doubt, fear, and insecurities into your relationship.
16. Do new and exciting things to keep your relationship enjoyable.

6

UNFAMILIAR TERRITORY

I started a new job at the sheriff's department. I was so excited since I no longer had my daycare center. This was a new journey, and I was looking forward to it. I started a six-month training class to become a fully vested officer. I was nervous not knowing what was ahead of me. The first day of training was exhausting. It was like military training. I was challenged mentally, physically, and emotionally. The training was intense. If a cadet was not prepared for inspection by having their police equipment in order and our uniform professionally worn, everyone had to pay for that person's mistake.

The shooting, driving, and obstacle courses were overwhelming. I failed the shooting and driving courses because I was afraid. I had never shot a gun or driven crazy on the streets. I was angry because I had to start a new class in the middle of the quarter. It took a lot for me to accept that failure. In the past, fear had discouraged me from following my passions in life. Therefore, I had to make a decision: take the class or resign. With my strength and faith, I had the courage to repeat the class.

Another part of the training was to visit the Baltimore Morgue. That experience helped me to understand how precious life is and not to take it for granted. I couldn't allow my past fears of being bullied in school, low self-esteem, and worrying about what other people thought of me to stop me from moving forward. "Have not I commanded thee? Be strong and of a good courage; be not afraid, neither be thou dismayed: for the LORD thy God is with thee whithersoever thou goest" (Josh. 1:9). I was very successful in completing the class I had to repeat. In fact, I had a perfect score of 100 in all my courses.

Once I returned to my full-time position as a fully vested sheriff, I was amazed by how my training had prepared and equipped me to work with people in the community who had committed homicide, rape, and child abuse, to name a few crimes. My life changed tremendously from having power over my life to having power and control over others, which didn't feel good. When you wear a sheriff's uniform, people look at you as a threat. They feel intimidated and fearful for their lives. It was important that I didn't abuse my authority and that I treat everyone with respect, in spite of who they were or the choices they made. One of the hardest parts of my job was evicting families with children; to see that child looking me in my eyes with such innocence was difficult. I had children of my own, and it was heartbreaking for me because I couldn't change these children's situation. I would go home and hug my children, thanking God for His mercy and grace over my family. "And whatsoever ye do in word or deed, do all in the name of the Lord Jesus, giving thanks to God and the Father by him," (Col. 3:17).

I established great relationships with juvenile boys and girls. Many of them would express to me how life was complicated for them because they did not have a mother or father in the home. They did not have anyone to love and guide them. Some of their parents were strung out on drugs, and they had to sell drugs to care for their siblings and parents to survive. I couldn't believe there were so many young boys and girls known to the system from getting into trouble. I was impressed with how smart and intellectual most of them were. They just needed a chance to prove themselves and for someone to listen and care about them. These young people were more than their situation and how society viewed them. It was a blessing to talk with them and speak greatness over their lives to keep them encouraged. "And be not conformed to this world: but be ye transformed by the renewing of your mind, that ye may prove what is that good, and acceptable, and perfect, will of God," (Rom. 12:2).

Please don't give up on our young people. They need constant guidance, support, and love. The media shows youth in a negative light, which causes them to be judged and stereotyped by the world. You have to hear their stories to know why they made the wrong choices for their lives. Society has created a system to keep our children programmed through social media, music, and game systems, which distracts them from manifesting their dreams and aspirations in life. We are living in a world where killing one another, incarnation, instant gratification, drugs abuse, selfishness, greed, and disrespect for themselves and others

Please don't give up on our young people. They need constant guidance, support, and love. The media shows youth in a negative light, which causes them to be judged and stereotyped by the world.

are the norm. They don't realize their true value. They alter their bodies from what God created. We have to rebuild our communities around the world to create an environment for them to work in their gifts and talents. This will keep them off the streets and out of trouble. We need to build career centers that prepare them to reach their full potential in becoming great leaders of the world.

Jewels to Live By:

1. Always remember, no matter how many times you fail or make a mistake, never compromise your confidence or give up.

2. Believe in yourself and go through the process because most of the time we are stronger than we think.

3. Defeat isn't an option. "God is our refuge and strength, a very present help in trouble." (Ps. 46:1).

7

SPIRITUAL ATTACKS AT WORK

The sheriff's department was a devilish environment to work in. Every sin was committed, i.e., adultery, betrayal, lying, and disloyalty. There was no way I was going to allow them to break my character by having my integrity questioned or compromised. However, things got worse. The supervisors abused their power and authority for personal gain by violating rules and regulations in the department. We officers were demoted for unfound reasons, and we were treated unfairly. Most of the female officers had their own social clique. They accused me of getting special privileges by sleeping around with supervisors. The demands and all the issues within the department weighed heavily on me. My faith was tested. The Devil used others to try to destroy my destiny and my character. I felt like a prisoner at work. It was a spiritual attack against me. "No weapon that is formed against thee shall prosper; and every tongue that shall rise against thee in judgment thou shalt condemn" (Isa. 54:17).

Jewels To Live By:

1. Seek God first before applying for any job.
2. Research the company.
3. Research the culture of the company.
4. See what other employees say about the company.
5. Research the company to see if they have a high turnover rate.
6. Check the history of the company.
7. Determine if you will be able to utilize your gifts and talents within the company.
8. Make sure that it is a good match for you and your family.
9. Research if there is career advancement available in the company.
10. Make sure you enjoy the job you will be doing.
11. Always stand up for what you believe in.
12. Don't use your position to hurt others for personal gain.
13. Stand tall through the fire with faith and prayer knowing that God will give you the victory!

*Stand tall through the
fire with faith and prayer
knowing that God will give
you the victory!*

8

UNFORESEEN CROSSROADS

On July 5, 2013, I was injured while restraining a juvenile who was trying to escape from a building. I injured my back trying to take him to the ground. On June 6, 2013, I went back to work, even though my doctor advised me not to because of severity of the injuries I sustained at work. I was frustrated, angry, feeling defeated, and fearful of losing my job. That was the last thing I wanted to hear. I was in disbelief after all I had been through in my career.

However, I was unable to do my job because of the pain, so I went back to my doctor. I was surprised when my doctor asked me if I watched much television. I said no and he said, "Get used to the remote. It's going to be your best friend." My life was turned upside down. I couldn't control what happened to me and didn't understand why God was allowing it to happen. I cried myself to sleep every night for almost a year because of the excruciating pain, until I had my back surgery. My recovery process lasted more than two years. I was unable to bathe myself, do any household chores, cook, or do grocery shopping without assistance.

Life wasn't fair! I felt like a failure to myself and my children. I had to pull my son out of private school because I couldn't afford the tuition. I couldn't do any fun outside activities with my children. I went from serving eviction notices to receiving them. We stopped praying and eating together as a family. My children begin having physical altercations with each other because they were filled with so much anger. I had to get on public assistance and receive financial help from family and friends for us to survive because my work-man's compensation benefits had ended. I felt so over-whelmed. I had to get my family back in order. The adversary was trying to destroy me and stop the love, joy, and peace between me and my family.

A week later, my mom had a stroke. I had to care for her and my children, which led me into depression. I had to find the strength, faith, and courage to keep going. Therefore, I started praying to God and attending church more regularly. God answered my prayers. In December 2014, I was awarded my medical disability retirement. "And God is able to make all grace abound toward you; that ye, always having all sufficiency in all things, may abound to every good work" (2 Cor. 9:8).

Jewels to Live By:

1. There's no such thing as failure, fear, or defeat. Those are issues we manifest within ourselves.
2. It's all in how we internalized what we go through.
3. It is imperative that we look within ourselves.
4. Through prayer and meditation, we can survive anything life throws our way.
5. Don't allow people, places, or situations to define who you are.
6. Trust the process. You will become unstoppable!

There's no such thing as failure, fear, or defeat. Those are issues we manifest within ourselves.

9

STAND IN YOUR TRUTH

On March 26, 2015, my children and I relocated to rebuild our lives. I was able to place my mother in a beautiful senior home with all the services she needed. It was an adjustment for my children to not see their friends because we moved so far away. I had to keep them grounded as a family. The adversary was trying to divide and destroy us. Our situation began to turn around gradually. They were doing well in school and adjusting to the new environment. But as we were getting on track, we were spiritually attacked again. " For we wrestle not against flesh and blood, but against principalities, against powers, against the rulers of the darkness of this world, against spiritual wickedness in high places," (Eph. 6:12).

One Saturday evening, I was on my way to pick up my two young teenage sons from the movies. I received a phone call that they were arrested. My heart was beating fast with so much anxiety. I was so afraid! That was the same time that the Freddie Gray case was happening. When I arrived at the police station, one of my sons' faces was filled with blood and bruises because the officers stomped him in his face. My other son had bruises on his face and forehead. It was painful knowing they were physically and verbally abused. I couldn't wake up from that terrible nightmare. My sons were violated. I couldn't protect them from that tragic situation.

I lost a part of my sons. They stop smiling and became very disrespectful to me and authority. They were acting out in school and becoming a lot for me to handle. I tried keeping them encouraged with love, prayer, and support. Praying to God just didn't seem like enough. It was a struggle for me as a mother and daughter. I was being pulled in so many different directions. If a woman says that she can raise a boy without a man, it isn't true. You really have to understand the crossroads they encounter and their emotions, attitudes, and mindsets. Ever since my medical disability, the adversary was on our trail. "⁵ Trust in the LORD with all thine heart; and lean not unto thine own understanding.⁶ In all thy ways acknowledge him, and he shall direct thy paths," (Prov. 3:5-6).

> *If a woman says that she can raise a boy without a man, it isn't true. You really have to understand the crossroads they encounter and their emotions, attitudes, and mindsets.*

With so much evil and violence in the world, we're not always in the position to protect to our children when they are not in our care. There are so many teenagers and children who experience physical, mental, verbal, and sexual abuse that causes them to become powerless and unable to protect themselves. This causes confusion in their thoughts and emotions, which leads to anger, low self-esteem, resentment, anxiety, and depression. They lose their sense of value as an individual. Give them love, support, and please seek help. They may never recover from the experience without it. They are a vital instrument to society and our communities around the world. They are the future of this generation. "Give instruction to a wise man, and he will be yet wiser: teach a just man, and he will increase in learning" (Prov. 9:9).

Jewels to Live By:

1. Trust the process.
2. Be aware of the adversary's tricks and schemes.
3. Don't allow the adversary to tear down your family structure.
4. Stay in constant prayer.
5. Fight back with God's Word.
6. The adversary uses busyness as a weapon to rob families of their time together with God.

The Poem "Sons Of The Nation"

SONS of our nation, wake up! SONS, too many of our young men of all cultures are being killed. SONS, there are too many single mothers raising young men alone because FATHERS aren't in the homes or involved in their lives. You are projecting emotions of anger through disrespect to your mothers, your queens. SONS, stand up to become great leaders and set goals of having a plan in place for your future. SONS of this nation, you are the life coaches. SONS, stop allowing social media networks, games, music, and cell phones to dictate your life. Allow love, care, and compassion to influence your mind. You cannot continue to disrespect yourselves and others. SONS, don't you know that the

---

SONS, stop allowing social media networks, games, music, and cell phones to dictate your life. Allow love, care, and compassion to influence your mind.

48

world is only creating an illusion to distract you from your higher gifts, talents, and purpose that God has for your lives? It's not just about being a great football player, basketball player, or rapper; that just limits you from becoming the true leader you are called to be. SONS, we need more engineers, school teachers, politicians, mentors, and entrepreneurs! Empower yourselves with self-esteem, not with sex, money, greed, drugs, and alcohol which cause you to self-destruct. Why? Because, SONS of our nation, I need you to love yourself and others. Why? Because you are important, SONS! Set the example that is strongly needed in this nation! This nation is at war, but victory first begins with you. Fight the demons within yourselves and do what's right. Don't continue to walk around in pain, screaming on the inside, wanting to be heard. Release that emotion of abandonment. You are not lost. Do not lose yourself. Care about your life. SONS, you are loved! SONS of this nation, becoming a man isn't just about being a provider of material possessions; it's about you being an example for the generations coming behind you! Show them how to be good businessmen in our nation and in our streets. Show this nation your worth, because your worth is more than being killed or being in jail. You are God-fearing leaders, engineers, lawyers, and doctors. Stop jeopardizing your freedom and future by committing crimes. Allow this nation to see how smart, gifted, and talented you are. Don't be trapped in society's prejudices. Mothers and Fathers of this nation, praise our sons for the positive choices they make. SONS of this nation, please put God and prayer back into your family and communities. Stop selling drugs, killing, robbing, sex trafficking, or anything else that is illegal or immoral. Be the warriors of this nation that God has called you to be! SONS of this nation, let your voice be heard. "Depart from evil, and do good; seek peace, and purse it," (Ps. 34:14). Nothing is impossible with God! Through faith, prayer, patience, and support, you can impact the world. Today, my sons are doing great, and I am very proud of them!

10

Uncomfortable Places

January 2018 was a new year for a new beginning for myself. Being retired did not provide enough income for me. My sons were preparing to graduate from high school, and my daughter was in cosmetology school. It was time for me to focus on my dreams and aspirations. Therefore, I attended business conferences, and I started a t-shirt business. I was content moving forward with my visions and plans. We were all in a good place in our lives. There was no confusion, trials, or tribulations.

Three months later, we had a fire in our condo apartment. The fire caused flooding and a lot of damage to our home. It was so surreal that this was happening to us. Especially when everything was going so great in our lives! We were displaced and had to live in a hotel. I didn't have the energy to handle another situation under those circumstances. I began drinking every day. I was not sleeping or eating. However, I found the strength to continue my motivational speaking to the youth and attended positive events to keep myself grounded. I refused to allow the situation to defeat me.

On March 22, 2018, I had a job interview at the hotel where we were living. I got the job as a houseman. It was an exciting time. I really needed more income. After working about six months, my mom's health began to decline. I didn't know if this was another spiritual attack. But, in spite of it all, I knew God had me here to fulfill His purpose. I had to keep pushing, but it was becoming difficult to maintain the position at the hotel. This vicious cycle had to stop. I needed a breakthrough. It was confusing. Again, I didn't know what God was doing in my life. This situation was too much to bear. "Peace I leave with you, my peace I give unto you: not as the world giveth, give I unto you. Let not your heart be troubled, neither let it be afraid" (John 14:27).

Working as a houseman at the hotel was a big adjustment for me. It was different from the type of jobs I was used to having. I never imagined I would be cleaning up behind people every day! Taking out loads of trash, cleaning toilets, and mopping floors felt beneath me. I have a great respect for people who clean for living.

Suddenly, fear came into my life. On October 7, I received a disturbing phone call from my daughter's father stating that she was in a terrible car accident and she was in a hospital in Washington D.C. The accident nearly killed her and her friends. I was in disbelief trying to remain calm. When I arrived at the hospital, I was filled with so much pain inside. Seeing her in that conditions made me want to scream and cry. She was my first born. I couldn't lose her. She had several pieces of glass in her face, and her arm was broken. The doctors said she may be paralyzed and never walk again. My heart was racing inside, and my anxiety got worse.

I didn't know how to think or feel. I was numb inside. I was angry, sad, and frustrated with God. This situation had me outraged! With my family and friends' support, I was able to hold on to my faith and believe that she would pull through this traumatic situation. Both of her dads were amazing. They stood by her side with love and support. They made sure that she had everything she needed.

I watched over her every night. I was thinking about all the memories we shared together. I knew we would continue making more memories. When she looked into my eyes, I kept a smile on my face, so she would continue to fight for her future. Unfortunately, I had to stop working at the hotel to care for my daughter, so she could live a normal life again. Her recovery was a painful process for her and our family. However, three months after her accident, she was able to walk on her own. She could use her arm again. Her face was healed completely, and she was as beautiful as she always was. My daughter is now doing great. She is a hairstylist, a phlebotomist, and an eyelash technician.

Jewels to Live By:

When God wants you to grow, He makes your life uncomfortable. Therefore, trust His plan for your life. You may need to change how you perceive situations and people in your life.

1. Don't compare yourself to others.
2. Don't rely on others for approval.
3. Don't seek validation from others to know who you are.
4. Don't use alcohol, drugs, or sex to help you cope with the challenges of life.
5. Seek help, and don't isolate yourself.
6. Talk to God about how you feel.
7. Always love yourself unconditionally.

When God wants you to grow, He makes your life uncomfortable. Therefore, trust His plan for your life.

About the Author

Minoka Smith is the mother of three adult children, an author, a motivational speaker, a youth mentor, a makeup artist, and a former Baltimore City Sheriff and daycare owner.

She has style, class, strength, and grace. She is also a humanitarian. She has spent most of her life teaching young adults to believe in themselves, to be their best, and to reach their full potential.

She gives God all the glory and praise for the transformation He did in her life.

She hopes this book will help other people overcome their adversities and discover the purpose God has for their life.

CPSIA information can be obtained
at www.ICGtesting.com
Printed in the USA
FFHW022159161219
57053497-62640FF

9 781630 501907